FAMILIES AROUND THE WORLD

A family from

VIETNAM

Simon Scoones

WAYLAND

FAMILIES AROUND THE WORLD

A family from **BOSNIA**

A family from **BRAZIL**

A family from **CHINA**

A family from **ETHIOPIA**

A family from **GERMANY**

A family from **GUATEMALA**

A family from **IRAQ**

A family from **JAPAN**

A family from **SOUTH AFRICA**

A family from **VIETNAM**

The family featured in this book is an average Vietnamese family. The Nguyens have been chosen because they are typical of the majority of Vietnamese families in terms of income, housing, number of children and lifestyle.

Cover: The Nguyen family outside their home with all their possessions.
Title page: Canh carries crops picked in the fields near her home.
Contents page: Villagers cycle to work in the paddy fields.

Series editor: Katie Orchard
Book editor: Alison Cooper
Designer: Tim Mayer
Production controller: Carol Titchener

Picture Acknowledgements: All the photographs in this book were taken by Leong Ka Tai. The photographs were supplied by Material World/Impact Photos and were first published in 1994 by Sierra Club Books in *Material World: A Global Family Portrait* © Copyright Peter Menzel/Material World. The map artwork on page 4 was produced by Peter Bull.

First published in 1998 by Wayland Publishers Limited
61 Western Road, Hove
East Sussex, BN3 1JD, England

© Copyright 1998 Wayland Publishers Limited

Find Wayland on the Internet at http://www.wayland.co.uk

Typeset by Mayer Media
Printed and bound in Italy by G. Canale & C.S.p.A., Turin.

British Library Cataloguing in Publication Data
Scoones, Simon
   A family from Vietnam. – (Families around the world)
   1. Family – Vietnam – Juvenile literature
   2. Vietnam – Social life and customs – Juvenile literature
   I. Title
   306.8'5'09597

ISBN 0 7502 2028 7

Contents

★ Introduction

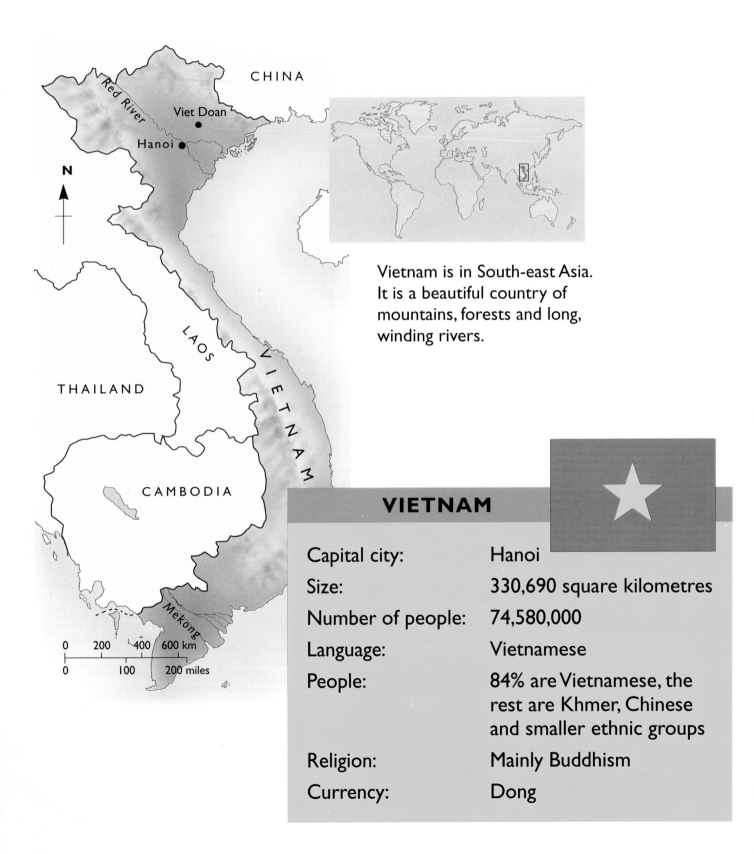

Vietnam is in South-east Asia. It is a beautiful country of mountains, forests and long, winding rivers.

VIETNAM

Capital city:	Hanoi
Size:	330,690 square kilometres
Number of people:	74,580,000
Language:	Vietnamese
People:	84% are Vietnamese, the rest are Khmer, Chinese and smaller ethnic groups
Religion:	Mainly Buddhism
Currency:	Dong

THE NGUYEN FAMILY

Size of household:	5 people
Size of home:	80 square metres
Work week:	119 hours (adults)
Most valued possessions:	Ha: His bicycle Hung: His football
Income for each family member:	About US$285 each year

The Nguyen family (you say 'Un-goo-wen') is an ordinary Vietnamese family. They have put everything that they own outside their home so that this photograph could be taken.

Meet the family

1 Ha, father, 33	4 Hung, son, 7
2 Canh, mother, 31	5 Hai, daughter, 3
3 Huong, daughter, 9	

Family Life

The Nguyen family lives in a small village called Viet Doan in the north of Vietnam. Many of their relatives live close by. The Nguyens' house is often bustling with lots of visitors.

Helping Out

The children's grandmother visits the family every day. She loves looking after her grandchildren. She knows exactly what to do, because she had ten children of her own. Ha and Canh are happy to have just three children.

'I have five brothers and sisters, and Ha has nine. Today, it is too expensive to have so many children.' *Canh*.

At home

Ha's family have lived in this house for many years.

A Family Home

Ha is very proud of his family's house. It was built many years ago by his grandparents. Vietnamese people like to live in the places where their ancestors lived before them. That way, they feel closer to them.

The house has everything that the family needs. It has one main room and a storage room. The living room is where the family gets together to eat, talk and sleep. Canh and Ha share one bed with Hai, their younger daughter. It is a tight squeeze, as Hai is growing very quickly. Hung and Huong share the other bed. Hung often complains when his sister takes all the covers.

Ha helps Huong with her homework at the living-room table.

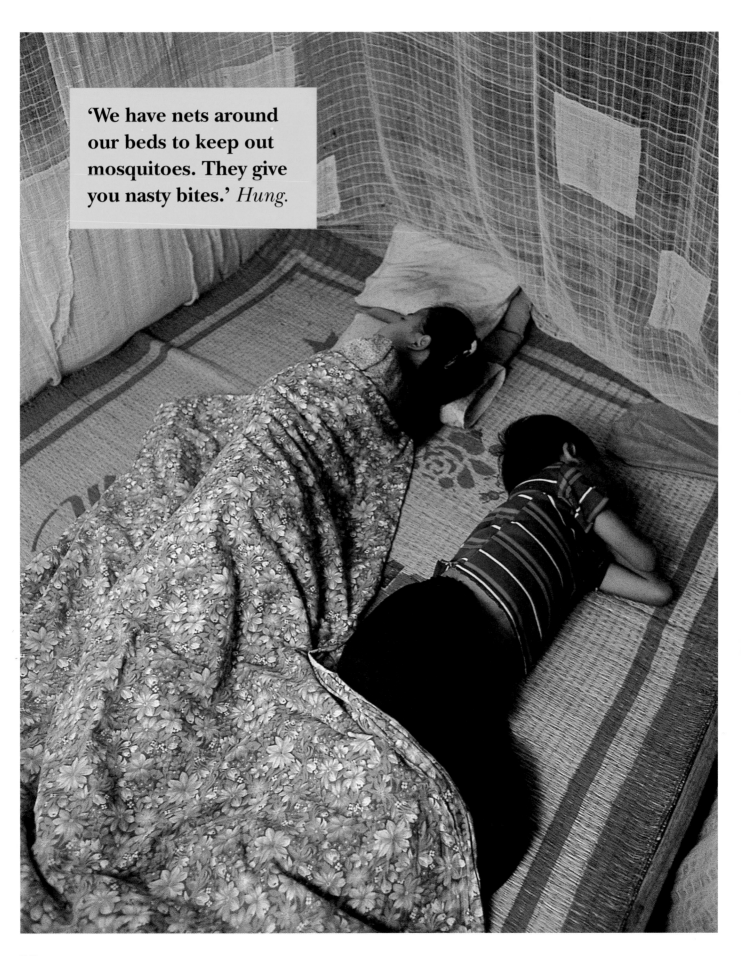

'We have nets around our beds to keep out mosquitoes. They give you nasty bites.' *Hung.*

In the Yard

Outside the house, there is a big back yard. Here, the family stores hay, and keeps some chickens so that there are fresh eggs to eat. Huong and Hung take turns to feed the chickens twice a day. The children like to play in the back yard too.

'Sometimes, the chickens creep into the house. Mum is always chasing them outside.' *Huong*.

Huong likes to watch the chickens scratching for food in the back yard.

Food and cooking

UNUSUAL DISHES

There are many different kinds of Vietnamese food, with over 500 interesting dishes to choose from. Some of these dishes are quite unusual. Some restaurants in the cities serve steamed snake and fried gecko, a type of lizard.

Canh puts the food into small bowls and serves the meals on big metal trays.

In the garden, Ha grows most of the vegetables that his family needs. They do not have a fridge, so Canh goes to the market every day to buy the food that they can't grow themselves.

12

Cooking Breakfast

Canh makes sure that everyone eats three good meals a day. For breakfast, she cooks a strong, spicy soup called *Pho*. Canh uses the meat juices left over from the meal the night before. Then she adds noodles, vegetables, lime, chillies and fish sauce.

Canh usually cooks outside in the back yard, where there is plenty of space for all the pots and pans.

Eating Together

At lunch time and dinner time Canh puts the food into little plates and bowls. Everyone has a bowl for rice, and usually another one for soup. There is a bowl of water too, so that the family can clean their fingers while they are eating. Everyone uses chopsticks to pick up food from the different dishes and put it in their rice bowls.

'During the evening meal, we tell the rest of the family about our day.' *Ha.*

'Hai likes to play with the water while she is washing the vegetables.' *Canh.*

'When the children grow up, it will be difficult to squeeze us all in!' *Ha.*

The whole family sits on the floor to eat, which makes it easier to fit everyone in.

Special Occasions

The Nguyens and their relatives always like to eat together on special occasions, such as festivals and public holidays.

Canh goes to the market with her mother and sisters. They usually buy some chickens or a large fish. The other relatives help by cooking more food, and everyone shares the dishes they have brought. The children always get excited because the house is full of people talking, laughing and eating.

'I like chatting to the market traders. I ask them to save the best chickens for me!' *Canh*.

Working hard

Although Ha works very hard, he makes sure that he spends some time with his children.

GROWING RICE

More than half of the people in Vietnam are farmers, and rice is the most important crop. Rice needs lots of water to grow, so farmers dig channels to carry water to their fields. The flooded rice fields are called paddies.

An Early Start

Everyone in the Nguyen family has a job to do. Hung gets up at five o'clock in the morning to feed the chickens. If they have laid any eggs, he gives them to his mother to use in the breakfast soup. Huong gets her little sister ready for nursery school.

Work in the Fields

The villagers work together so that everyone can have a good rice harvest.

Ha and Canh go to work when the sun rises, and return home after dark. Canh grows rice with the other villagers. It is very hard work, but they all help each other. Before she plants the rice, Canh uses her neighbour's water buffalo to churn the paddy field into a muddy soup. Then she floods the field with water. When the rice is ripe, Canh cuts the plants with a knife, so that she can collect the grains of rice from them.

This machine is used to polish the grains of rice and make them clean.

Supplying Water

Ha works at a pumping station. He has to make sure that the pumps supply enough water to the ditches and canals around the local rice paddies. Ha works very long hours.

Earning Enough

Ha always cycles to work because it's too far to walk.

Ha and Canh make just enough money to keep the family well fed. Sometimes, they have a little extra to buy some new clothes for the children, or some school books for Huong and Hung.

School and play

Huong helps her mother by taking Hai to the nursery school each day.

EDUCATION

Education is very important in Vietnam. Almost all Vietnamese children can read and write. Even though it is a poor country, many older students save up to go to university.

Huong and Hung go to the primary school near their home. Hai has just started going to the nursery school. It does not take them long to walk there but Huong usually gives Hai a piggyback because she is still too young to walk that far.

'I like walking to school with my friends.' *Hung.*

There are forty children in Huong's class.

After School

Huong always works very hard at school. She wants to do well in her exams next year, and hopes she will get a good job when she is older. Every night Huong spends a long time doing her homework.

Hung does not have to do much homework yet. He can spend more time playing with his friends. Hung loves playing football. He also likes collecting insects and racing them against each other.

'One day, I want to be in the Vietnam football team – it's one of the best teams in Asia!' *Hung.*

Spare time

The Nguyens like to spend public holidays with their relatives.

There are many festivals in Vietnam. One of the most important festivals is *Tet*, when Vietnamese people celebrate New Year. People pray in pagodas and prepare special family feasts. They also let off loud firecrackers to celebrate.

Time to Relax

The family does not have much free time, but everyone makes the most of it. Canh practises an ancient Chinese pastime called *Tai ji*. It helps her to stretch all her muscles after a hard day's work. Huong and Hung like to watch the television at their uncle's house.

Days Out

Hanoi, the capital city of Vietnam, is only an hour away from Viet Doan by bus. On public holidays, the Nguyens sometimes go there with their relatives to see a puppet show. They also like to walk around the beautiful lake in the middle of the city. The adults visit a pagoda to pray.

Hung and Huong spend a lot of time playing together.

'Hung is always collecting things! I help him to find new bits and pieces.' *Huong.*

The future

Many Vietnamese people now use motorbikes, instead of bicycles, to get around.

A CHANGING COUNTRY

Until recently, Vietnam was one of the poorest countries in the world. But it is changing very fast. Some farmers are moving to the big cities to take up new jobs in factories and hotels. Many foreign businesses are moving to Vietnam, too.

Everyone in the Nguyen family hopes that their lives will be easier in the future. Ha would like to buy a motorbike. Huong wants to become a teacher. If Hung is not good enough for the Vietnam football team, he hopes to get a job in one of the new hotels in Hanoi.

'In the past, my country fought many wars. I hope that Vietnam will always be a peaceful place in the future.' *Huong.*

29

Timeline

200 BC	China invades Vietnam and rules it for over 1,000 years.
AD 1858	The French invade Vietnam and divide the country in half.
1945	Ho Chi Minh becomes the new leader of North Vietnam. He declares the country independent.
1965	The USA invades Vietnam to protect the government of South Vietnam from Ho Chi Minh's army in the north.
1976	North and South Vietnam become one country again, and the Vietnamese people start rebuilding their lives.
1994	President Clinton agrees that Vietnam and the USA should trade again. Many US companies open offices and factories in Vietnam.

Glossary

Ancestors Members of a family who lived and died many years ago.

Buddhism Religious beliefs developed by the Buddha, a religious leader from India.

Chillies Small, very spicy vegetables.

Chopsticks A pair of thin sticks that people use to pick up food.

Ethnic group People who share the same language, religion and traditions.

Independent To be free from the control of other countries.

Khmer People who come from Cambodia, a country near Vietnam, in South-east Asia.

Mosquitoes Small insects that bite.

Noodles A dried food, made from flour. It is rather like spaghetti.

Pagodas Buildings where people go to worship.

Pumping station A building in which pumps are set up to move water from one place to another.

Stilts Long posts that are used to raise buildings off the ground.

Tai ji An ancient type of exercise which is meant to help the body and mind.

Water buffalo A large, strong animal from southern Asia. It is a bit like

Further information:

Books to read:

Books for younger readers about Vietnam are difficult to find. You might like to read *I Come From Vietnam* by Jo Matthews (Watts, 1993).

Organizations:

The following organizations have a selection of education packs with case studies of children around the world:

Action Aid, Chataway House, Chard, Somerset TA20 1FA Tel: 01460 62972

Oxfam, 274 Banbury Road, Oxford OX2 7DZ Tel: 01865 311311

Index